THE LITTLE BOOK OF GHOST STORIES

True tales from trusted sources

ALEX KLAUSHOFER

First published as an e-book by Hermes Books in 2022. This paperback edition published in 2023.
Copyright © Alex Klaushofer 2022.
The moral right of the author has been asserted.

All rights reserved. No part of this publication may be reproduced, stored in a retrieval system, or transmitted, in any form or by any means, without the prior written permission of the publisher, except for brief excerpts in reviews and articles.

ISBN 978-0-993323638
Hermes Books
www.alexklaushofer.com

CONTENTS

Introduction	v
Part I: Unholy spirits	1
1. Beached bones	2
2. A night-time visitor	6
Part II: Spooky businesses	10
3. Sleepless in Bridgnorth	11
4. A Cotswold adventure	13
5. Playtime at the inn	19
Part III: Spirit of place	23
6. Murder at the mill	24
7. The choking hand	27
8. Pistols at dawn	29
Part IV: Quantum times	32
9. Alice in Spiritland	33
10. Historical slips	38
11. Old woman knitting	41
12. After-death appearances	43
Part V: And finally ...	49
13. The ghost's tail	50
About the author	51

INTRODUCTION

The ghost stories in this collection are absolutely true.

It's a bold statement, I know, so I'll explain further. The stories that follow are true in the sense that they are all genuine accounts, told to me in good faith, by people I believe to be trustworthy. They are testimony to a broader understanding of truth than that the one which has dominated the western world over the past couple of centuries. Viewed from within the framework of scientific materialism, the super-natural (literally 'above the natural') cannot be verified by the senses and is thus unproven at best, erroneous at worst. But human life has always had elements of mystery, and people have always shared their experiences, whether by talk or tale. The supernatural inhabits a realm of human experience common to all times and places.

The relegation of ghosts to the margins in our times has led them to resurface, in grand form, in the field of entertainment. In modern culture, ghost stories abound in novels, young adult fiction, films and TV programmes, images and memes. Safely inhabiting the realm of fiction, they challenge nothing in our everyday experience or the accepted beliefs of our age.

Growing up in a big Victorian house in the 1970s, I was as susceptible to the fear of these manufactured ghosts as the next child. I didn't like going upstairs alone and would rush, eyes averted, past the dark part of the landing. But the family home was not, as far as I could tell, haunted: never once did I see or hear anything that gave substance to those fears. Decades later after the house had been sold, I sometimes had a curious sense of being in the hall, floating about a foot off the floor, able to apprehend the colour and texture of the wall. I wondered if I might be a kind of ghost, and if the current occupants of the house had any sense of my presence.

Since then, I've become increasingly aware that human experience is far greater and more complex than is often imagined - and that, if we are prepared to listen and feel with curiosity, it can open up in extraordinary ways.

The stories in this volume were told to me by someone I know, or are set in a place I know well, or both. They were collected over a number of years in an organic fashion, arising out of my own experience or in the course of happenstance conversation. A couple are modern fireside tales, told to a circle gathered round an outdoors fire. All take place in southern England and Wales, the part of the world I know best. In that sense, they are stories of place, viewed from another angle.

In many cases, I've had the opportunity to follow up on the original telling and been able to check some details or hear a second account. But some stories I heard just once or found the teller unable to expand further. These slighter accounts are offered as just what they are: slithers of human experience, glimpses of another way of seeing. With one exception, the names of people have been changed. But the names of places, when given, are accurate.

The stories are gathered into loose thematic groups. The first two highlight the uneasy relationship the Christian church has with the supernatural, while another group attests to the reputation of hotels and inns for hauntings. Others speak to the close connection between place and people, the past and the present, and the living and the dead.

I retell them here as a secondhand chronicler, a role perhaps somewhere between a reporter and a storyteller in the oral tradition. Whatever the case, I've tried to be a good listener, accepting what I hear without seeking to allocate it to a binary true-or-false position. I hope they make you wonder.

PART I: UNHOLY SPIRITS

The following two stories were told to me by people I've known most of my life and the events they record occurred in places that were part of my growing up. They illustrate how the ecclesiastical discomfort of the Christian church when confronted with the supernatural has sometimes tipped into suppression.

I

BEACHED BONES

The fear of disturbing the dead and the consequences of not respecting their remains is a common one. This account concerns a beach I've visited many times, but until I heard it I was unaware of the shipwrecks that form part of the history of the Pembrokeshire coast. After the first telling, the teller supplied me with a written version and the following reflects the style of the original story.

After her retirement in the early 1990s, Margaret moved to the tiny cathedral city of St David's and set about establishing herself in her new community. As an active member of the Church of England, she was drawn to the life that revolved around the cathedral, with its many societies and activities. At the Mother's Union (a Christian version of the Women's Institute), the elderly Kay took her under her wing and from then on, the two women sat next to each other in the meetings held each month in one of the cathedral buildings.

Kay lived nearby in a house owned by the church, but the cathedral lay in a deep hollow and moving between its surrounding buildings involved negotiating steep slopes. As the months went on, she found the walk to the meeting increasingly arduous. One day, she arrived just as the meeting was starting. 'Well, I'm here at last,' she said as she sank into the chair next to Margaret. 'It's becoming a mighty hill to climb. The old bones are rattling away!'

'Shhh!' said the chairman. 'We are about to say the Mother's Union prayer!'

Both women immediately stopped talking and the meeting got underway.

Afterwards, Kay turned to Margaret. 'Come home and have a drink with me. I have something to tell you.'

Ten minutes later, the two friends were sitting in the garden with glasses of homemade lemonade, and Kay began her story.

It was six o'clock on a bright spring morning. Kay had woken early, but it was impossible to go back to sleep. The birds were singing and the outside world was beckoning; beyond the green cradle of the cathedral close the open spaces of sea and sky were ablaze with first light. She decided she would go to Whitesands, a favourite beach of hers that was just a short drive away. She got up, dressed quickly and went downstairs to the garage, pausing only to grab a couple of biscuits from the kitchen.

Whitesands Beach was a long stretch of pale sand that was a perfect setting for contemplating the ocean. But it was the grassy lowlands behind the shoreline that caught Kay's eye: they were abloom with wild flowers. Entranced, she made her way towards them: close up they were primroses. How sweet the flower-faces of delicate yellow would look in her tiny front garden! She decided to pop home, pick up a basket and trowel and return to dig up half a dozen roots. She knew it was illegal to take flowers from the wild: the deed could bring her a hefty fine and publicity that would damage her standing in the church community. But her desire for the flowers was overwhelming.

A short while later, she was back among the primroses. It was no easy task, crouching down and loosening the soil around the plants while scanning the horizon for unwanted observers. But finally she had unearthed six good specimens with healthy roots. She laid them in the basket and covered them with a cloth, carefully refilling the holes in the ground with grassy soil. Then she hurried back to the car.

The cathedral clock was striking seven-thirty when Kay arrived home, and the canon was crossing the close on his way to Morning Prayer. 'Kay!' he shouted. 'Whatever brings you out so early? Did you hear me singing "Awake, my soul and with the Sun?" It's good to sing while you are shaving!'

The canon often dropped by for a cup of tea between duties, so Kay decided not to plant the stolen primroses that day in case he should catch her. They would keep well enough in the coolness of the garage until all was quiet on the cathedral close.

But that night, her sleep was riven by a powerful nightmare. 'Kay,' a voice seemed to say. 'Among the primrose roots you dug up were human bones. You will be cursed. Take them back to where you found them. It is holy ground.'

She awoke, shaken to the core. It was barely dawn, but she had no doubt about what to do. She got up, dressed quickly and went downstairs to the garage. Her fingers were trembling as she reached for the basket in the dark; it tipped, and the plants fell out onto the floor. Hastily, she scooped them back into the basket and got into the car.

Thankfully, there was no one else on the beach as she made her way to the spot where she had dug up the primroses. As she lifted the plants from the basket and carefully set them back into the ground, her fingers felt something hard. She peered into the mess of roots and earth: three small pieces of bone lay among the soil. Kay sat back on her haunches and shook for a long time.

After that, Kay did her best to forget her strange experience. But when her house was inspected a few years later, the church authorities decided to repaint the garage doors inside and out. In the course of the work, some human bones were found in the dust on the floor. They were taken away for examination and found to be those of a small baby.

For a while, there was speculation among the church community about the origins of the bones from the beach. But soon enough, the talk died away and the matter was forgotten.

2

A NIGHT-TIME VISITOR

Cathy is one of my childhood friends and I was a frequent visitor to her house in the Gloucestershire village where we both grew up. This is the first true ghost story I remember hearing.

I was eleven when I met Cathy, who was a little older than me, after her family moved into a strange chalet of a house down the lane. The house had always felt sinister to me: set back from the road amid a tangle of shrubs, it was an odd-shaped construction of wooden boards stained the colour of black treacle. Inside it was dark and I hadn't liked calling on its previous occupant when collecting the village subscriptions to the Royal Society for the Protection of Animals, a charity job my mother thought good for me. The elderly Mrs Finlay would take ages to answer the door and then another age to find her purse. She would ask me to step inside while she shuffled around and I would stand in the dim hallway, taking in the piles of yellowed newspapers and the dark furniture that merged into the wooden floors and walls.

The new household transformed the atmosphere: it was now a family home resounding with her mother's high-pitched calls for her four-year-old, husband or Cathy's older sister. Some evenings I would escape my own quiet, chilly home to join the family as they crammed around the fire in the little living room. Upstairs was the domain of the two teenage girls, where Cathy and I would usually retreat. Her older sister had the bigger room and a record player; she'd invite us in to listen to listen to her latest record or hear about her current boyfriend, giggling as she implied what they'd got up to in the darkness of Gloucester arcade.

You couldn't do much in Cathy's room, an L-shape formed of a little passageway that turned sharply into a wooden space big enough only for a narrow bed and a chest of drawers. We would sit on the bed while Cathy applied her makeup, spitting into her block mascara and mixing up a black mess with a tiny brush. I didn't much like being in her room: it was cramped, dark and had a funny atmosphere. But it was the only place in the house where we could have a truly private conversation. We were at that stage of life when confidences passed between us as easily as water and I was intimately familiar with her concerns: the behaviour of the other teenagers in our village hang-outs, the bitchiness of the girls at the local comprehensive and her chances of love with the good looking boy-next-door.

But one concern was less typically adolescent. Cathy complained, repeatedly, of waking during the night to find a man staring at her. Sometimes he stood at the end of the bed, at others beside it. Sometimes he would bend forwards, apparently trying to get a better look at her. It was difficult to know how to respond to this particular confidence: the man never did anything more than stare, nor did Cathy seemed frightened he would try to. And while it was clear that he wasn't a burglar or stalker, he had none of the characteristics of ghosts I'd heard about; there was no blood or uncanny sounds. Cathy's problem was just a man standing and staring, a kind of cinematic fragment which played out in her bedroom night after night. What did he look like, I wanted to know? Middle-aged with mid-brown hair, was all she could offer. Not particularly tall.

Thanks to the porosity of the teenage psyche, I can still see the man in my mind's eye. His face was wide, low-browed, his expression somewhere between troubled and cross. He wasn't someone I'd want to speak to, but neither did he inspire fear. The predominant impression was of ordinariness. Yes, that was it: he was an ordinary man somehow caught up in a spooky situation. With hindsight, he seemed to be as puzzled by his presence in Cathy's bedroom as she was.

At the same time, part of me was quietly sceptical about Cathy's night-time sightings. Her emotional life seemed to be a series of mini-dramas while I, a year and a half younger, navigated duller but more tranquil waters. Was it possible she was simply 'seeing things'? No one else in her house was troubled by ghosts.

But the nocturnal visits continued, and Cathy decided to talk to the vicar. This would be easy enough: the two of us were preparing for confirmation, having assured our mothers that we were ready to become adult members of the Church. In the run-up to the service, we were having some sessions with the vicar to develop our understanding of the Bible and the main Christian beliefs. Consulting him about the ghost seemed a good plan: as well as being official spokesman for The Realm of the Unseen, he was a young, energetic man who took an active interest in the lives of his parishioners.

So one light evening in late spring as the three of us sat in the side-aisle of the village church, Cathy told the vicar about her disturbed nights. I can't remember how she put it, but I clearly recall his blue eyes widening with fear. 'Don't think about it,' he advised her hastily. 'That's the best way to deal with evil.' And then the conversation moved swiftly back to matters biblical.

I don't remember, either, exactly what we said to each other as we walked home that evening. I think we probably expressed a vague sense of disappointment at the failure of the adult world to provide an answer, but accepted that the mystery of what was going on and what to do about it remained with us, something apparently unsolvable. And then I suppose, we moved on the way children generally do. Gradually, the ghost disappeared behind the all-consuming concerns of adolescence and Cathy spoke of him no more.

PART II: SPOOKY BUSINESSES

I've heard it said that pubs and hotels are common sites for hauntings, partly because they are often old buildings with histories that inevitably involve some death and disaster. Perhaps the number of people passing through such places also helps the stories to spread. A common feature of the following three accounts is how the residents and staff of such places live alongside their ghosts and tolerate them, even while being irritated by their activities.

3

SLEEPLESS IN BRIDGNORTH

This story was told as a group of us sat around the fire in my back garden. Its teller was a sceptically-minded friend who often travelled around Britain in the course of his job in sales.

My friend had checked into a hotel in the Welsh borders where he sometimes stayed during the working week. That night, in the bar after dinner, he noticed that a fellow-resident was downing one whisky after another.

'Thirsty, aren't you, mate?' he teased him.

The man put his latest glass down on the bar with a glum expression. 'I'm trying to knock myself out,' he explained. 'Last night I hardly got any sleep. Every time I was on the point of dozing off, I felt something pulling on the duvet.'

He would switch the light on and it would stop. Then, as soon as he'd switched the light off and settled back down to sleep, the pulling would start again. Every time he put the light on, it would stop again. This went on for most of the night. Light off: tug, tug, tug. Light on: everything went still.

'I wasn't particularly scared.' The man took another slug of whisky. 'It didn't feel malicious or anything. It was more the kind of playful pulling that a child does when mucking about. But now, I'm really, really, tired and I want to get some sleep.'

My friend wished his fellow guest a good night's rest with more than the usual sincerity. He didn't see the other man again, but the next day he got chatting to a member of the hotel staff about what he'd heard.

It was well-known among the staff that the room where the sleep-deprived guest had been staying was haunted, said the employee, along with the one next door. Before their conversion into smaller hotel rooms, they had previously been one big room with a fireplace. It was said that, long ago, a child had fallen into the fire and had died as a result of her injuries.

❧ 4 ☙

A COTSWOLD ADVENTURE

It was summer in Gloucestershire. An old schoolfriend and I had 'come home' decades after leaving and were spending a few days' walking the Cotswold Way. We'd finished our hike for the day and were exploring Wotton-under-Edge before returning to her camper van. There was not much to see in the small Cotswold town after we'd peered into the shops on the High Street so, with hours of daylight ahead, we'd turned idly down a road that seemed to lead nowhere in particular.

'What's this?'

The writing in the filthy window almost spoke out loud. The words 'TV' and 'MOST HAUNTED' were scrawled across the paper in handwritten capitals.

Intrigued, we stopped to take a closer look. But the sign didn't make much sense, so we continued along the narrow pavement. The building that ran alongside it was in a lamentable state of repair and seemed to be sinking into the ground. A bulging half-timbered gable hung over the road and merged into a long low building, and then another. In one of the windows further along, someone had posted a piece of A4 headed 'Help save The Ancient Ram Inn'. 'If you are a paranormal team, see John at the start because there are those who have left unpaid,' added the text below. It was as if the signs were in conversation with the outer world. Next, came a newspaper article entitled: 'Things that go bump at the old Ram Inn'. Clearly, this strange building had drawn some media coverage.

There was another sign in a broken window. This was Britain's most haunted house, it declared. It was a thousand years old. Tours were possible. Everyone was welcome.

Bea and I exchanged looks. Should we?

Moments later, we were standing just inside a generous courtyard. At the far end was an L-shaped construction. One leg was the inside of the section that shadowed the pavement, the other was a substantial building with a set of white French doors. It was easy to imagine how, under different conditions, the house might have been a large family home of the kind you often see in wealthy parts of the Cotswolds. Or how, in its heyday as an inn, coaches would have turned into the space, disgorging tired travellers.

But the building in front of us was decidedly dilapidated. White plaster fell away to reveal dusty stonework and plants crept riotously up its sides. A lantern and a flagpole stood randomly in the yard. From within the house, came the sound of the early evening news, blaring away at high volume.

We stood hesitantly, wondering whether to announce ourselves or leave.

Then a small figure shuffled out, an old man with long white hair.

We drew nearer, smiling in the hesitant way of English women when they want something but don't want to be any trouble.

Of course we could have a tour.

Inside, the man's home was dark and cluttered. A kind of room-within-a-room had been created out of pieces of furniture: a narrow sofa, a large TV screen and some pieces of dark wood formed a three-sided snug into which we were invited. 'I do like to watch the news,' remarked the man conversationally as he sat down. 'I've been doing this all day.'

We joined him on the sofa, and a disjointed conversation between the three of us ensued. Speaking in a strong Gloucestershire accent, our host made a series of statements about the house and the life within it: it was a thousand years old, and was home to ghosts and spirits from different times. But the incubus was a problem. When he used to spend the night upstairs, it wouldn't let him sleep and would constantly try to interfere with him. He was better down here, sleeping on the sofa. The man ran his hands apologetically over his head. 'The incubus messes with your hair,' he explained.

Bea and I were politely puzzled. Neither of us could quite remember what an incubus was, but it certainly sounded bothersome.

'Why do you stay?' I wanted to know.

'My Christian faith is so strong,' the man replied simply.

'So can we have a look around?' asked Bea brightly.

Our host led us into the next room. Ramshackle pieces of furniture stood among bare stone walls and vivid red furnishings. 'Ooh, it's cold in here,' shivered Bea. 'There's a real drop in temperature.' A portion of the floor had been dug up, leaving a pit of exposed earth. A large wooden cross stood in the hole, and a skull and friendly-looking dragon toy looked on from the side. The remains of a woman and child had been found here, explained our guide; centuries ago, it had been the site of a pagan sacrifice.

The next room had clearly been the main saloon. A long wooden bar curled through a space littered with barrels, low velvet stools and tattered armchairs. The dark ceiling beams and fireplace were studded with brass horseshoes and vases of plastic flowers and china ornaments adorned little tables. 'The ghost of a crippled child is seen waving to passers by, here -' read a sign in blood-red capitals.

It was hard to know how to respond to this mixture of clutter and kitsch amid the evidence that this was a building which attracted interest from serious ghost hunters and paranormal investigators. It was clear from the signs and supernatural paraphernalia that its owner wanted to make the most of this interest and to give his visitors a spooky time. Yet he wasn't running a commercial enterprise and was clearly dedicated to the place; it wasn't so much his home as a vocation. We wondered aloud whether he had family nearby and were relieved to hear that the CCTV camera in one corner had been set up by his daughter to keep an eye on him. Was this a hammy house of faux-horrors, the home of a vulnerable old man, or a truly haunted house? Perhaps it was all three at the same time.

We peered into a barn containing a fridge, a motorbike and a long stack of furniture. Then the old man directed us up a twisting wooden staircase. The remains of children lay under it, he said, and a smoky human form sometimes appeared on the stairs themselves.

On the next floor, the window sill bore a host of ceramic ornaments: a hunter trotted by on his horse, oriental figures squatted under some giant china cats. 'The ghost of a very old lady appears here and moves out of the door and on to the landing seen by myself, my daughters and others,' announced a notice pinned onto the wood with a drawing pin.

Our guide opened a bedroom door and ushered us in. 'This is the Bishop's Room, the most haunted room in the house!' he said dramatically. Ghost hunting guests had often stayed there, sometimes running screaming from the room in the middle of the night. We stood, surveying the scene and trying to assess the atmosphere. The three beds had covers of the brightest scarlet and on each was a pile of cuddly toys. The bedside tables were coated with dust.

A loud banging made us jump. The old man was pounding the door with what looked like a bishop's crook.

Downstairs by the television, we thanked him and gave him a note for his trouble. Back out in the street, we exchanged knowing smiles with a woman outside the house opposite and then we made our way to where the van was parked, unsure about exactly what it was we'd experienced that afternoon.

All was green and peaceful in the farmer's field where we were camping. We had a simple supper and turned in for the night. Bea's van had a Goldilocks' cosiness: the bed was neither too big nor too small and the duvet was just right. I had slept well the past few nights.

But the next morning I struggled to resurface from currents of darkness;: I had had a powerful nightmare. So had Bea. Hers took a personal form: her house was unaccountably full of rowdy people and she wanted to get rid of them. She went to enlist the help of her husband but found him in the bath, awake but unresponsive. The next thing she knew he was standing in front of her, falling, falling, until he collapsed dead on the floor.

In my dream, I had come to the Ram Inn with a research group of some kind. We were coolly professional as we sat in the living room, but later that night, asleep in an upstairs room, I was jolted awake with an overwhelming sense of malevolence. I flew out of the house, ejected by what felt like a physical force, landing in the courtyard with a huge sense of relief and shouting to my colleagues in the building behind that they must get out too.

At home in London a couple of days later, I looked up the Ram Inn at Wotton-under-Edge on the internet. John Humphries, a former train driver, had bought the building from a brewery in 1968. Ever since, his life had centred around the struggle to preserve a building that he couldn't afford to maintain. His family had grown up there, but now he was the only one left.

We had indeed stumbled across Britains's most haunted house. In paranormal circles it was famous, variously dubbed the scariest building in England, no, Europe, no, the world. According to John Yates, who had been Bishop of Gloucester while Bea and I were growing up locally had called The Ram Inn the 'most evil place [he had] ever had the misfortune to visit'.

5

PLAYTIME AT THE INN

It was a mild winter's day in the West Country and I was meeting a friend for a walk, followed by lunch. It was my birthday and I'd chosen as destination Brown's Folly, a nineteenth century tower on the wooded slopes overlooking the road between Bradford-on-Avon and Bath. The tower was not particularly tall or architecturally significant, nor was its setting particularly beautiful. But I loved high places and had visited most of the high points within driving distance. Brown's Folly was the last on the list.

The tower did have one claim to interest: the woods in which it stood was known as Sally in the Wood, after the ghost of a woman who reportedly haunted the area.

Local stories told of a white-robed figure who appeared on the road at night and scared drivers into near or actual accidents. The accounts of who the woman had been varied: one had it that she'd been a servant in a big house who was got with a child by an aristocratic gentleman and then shut up in the tower without food or water until she died. Another told of a witch who had lived in the woods until she was a hundred. Such tales had often come to mind as I drove along the tree-shrouded road at night but I never saw anything. Nor, after several years living in the area, had I ever met anyone with direct experience of anything uncanny there.

Following some online directions, we drove to the village of Monkton Farleigh and parked in a lane. The tower wasn't easy to find, but after a tramp across a field and beating an overgrown path through the woods, there it was, a square of stone rising amid the trees. Evidently, not many people bothered to visit; the site had a neglected feel. A couple of crumpled lager cans lay amid the dead leaves. Looking up at the tower, I wondered whether it was worth climbing. But inside the atmosphere was bleak and the unrailed concrete steps jutted into empty space. Soon we turned back, hoping for an early lunch at a nearby pub, a handsome seventeenth century building that exuded affluence and ease.

Gavin and Chris had taken over the business just three weeks earlier and were brimming with enthusiasm for their new project. The pub had been closed for some time and the two men were looking forward to making it a focus for the community, somewhere with a welcoming atmosphere and a varied menu. But it had yet to re-establish itself in the minds of the locals and so far on that weekday winter lunchtime, we were the only customers. Gavin disappeared into the kitchen to prepare our food, while my friend and I installed ourselves by the open fire.

After we'd eaten, the two men leaned on the bar, ready for a chat. Gavin had grown up locally, playing in the quarry caves below Brown's Folly, so I asked him about Sally in the Wood. He shook his head: he'd never experienced anything unusual there. He paused, and added: 'This place has some funny stuff, though.'

At night especially, he sometimes heard the sound of children running around. Chris nodded in agreement. Moving some barrels in the cellar one evening, he'd heard a child say 'hello'. He said 'hello' back, and heard a giggle.

The first couple of nights, the couple had spent in the pub had been particularly lively. As they were closing up, things started to fly across the bar. Gavin gestured to one of the bottles behind him: 'The lid flew off and hit me on the head.' Another evening, he'd been in the bath when a two pence piece had hit him. 'Coins often fly about.'

On another occasion, parts of a lamp had flown off and hit some customers down the far end of the bar. They had asked Gavin what on earth he was doing, throwing things around like that. He'd told them that he hadn't touched the lamp and anyway, all its parts were firmly fixed on.

Both men were accustomed to coming down in the morning and finding that objects had been moved overnight. Things often went missing. 'They like packets of polos for some reason,' said Gavin. 'They often disappear.'

I was struck by the matter-of-fact way the men talked of their experiences and how they seemed to accept them as something that went with their new home and business. But I was even more surprised when Gavin revealed that he was a paranormal investigator. 'This stuff follows me around,' he said equably. 'I'm used to it.'

Chris, he added, didn't believe in ghosts. 'After all you've experienced.' He sent a nod of a reproach in his partner's direction. Chris shrugged. 'I just look for every other explanation first,' he replied.

As my friend and I put on our coats and prepared to leave, I mentioned my accidental visit to John Humphries at the Ram Inn. Gavin nodded. 'He's in a home now.'

At home that evening, looking up Gavin's paranormal site online, I came across a post saying that John Humphries had died the day before. I wondered what would become of the building he had carefully stewarded for decades, with its spirits and stories.

Six months later, I returned to the pub near the folly with another friend, hopeful of lunch. But the door was closed and a sign indicated that a change of management had taken place. We knocked and enquired, and were told by a young man that Gavin and Chris were now running a pub in Wiltshire.

PART III: SPIRIT OF PLACE

The following trilogy illustrates how deeply embedded local stories can become in the life of a particular place. Strictly speaking, tales told on ghost walks wouldn't qualify for inclusion in a volume such as this. But living or working in the places concerned has given me various opportunities to hear or experience things that lend them an extra layer of authenticity.

6

MURDER AT THE MILL

I heard this story from Jasper Bark as part of his ghost walk in Bradford-on-Avon. Like much of Wiltshire, the Cotswold town is rich in supernatural tales but I particularly like this account and the following story, The Choking Hand, for their contemporaneity. At the time of telling, we were standing in Greenland Mills, a housing development that has replaced the old wool factories on the southern bank of the River Avon.

In 2002, began Jasper, a new couple moved to Bradford-on-Avon. While they looked around for a property to buy, they rented a house here in Greenland Mills. As he spoke, I was acutely aware of the sound of the river rushing behind the narrow gabled houses. The darkness of this part of town seemed to heighten the other senses.

Late one night, Jasper went on, the woman – let's call her Meg – came back from an evening out and noticed an old woman was sitting on a wall on the other side of the close, apparently wearing a nightdress. Thinking she might be in trouble, Meg went to talk to her. Close to, the woman was younger than she first thought, perhaps in her late thirties, with long, dyed-blond hair. The nightdress she wore was soaking.

'I don't know where I am,' the woman told her. 'I can't rest.' She seemed confused.

'That's my house.' She pointed to the terrace opposite. Meg was surprised: she knew all the residents in the close but had never seen the woman before. Thinking that she was mentally disturbed or had perhaps taken some drugs, she offered to help her home.

But the blond woman shook her head. 'I can't rest,' she repeated. 'I can't go home. It's my husband, you see. He's ever so jealous.'

'But you're soaking,' protested Meg. In vain, she tried to persuade the woman to let her take her home. But the woman kept repeating the same things: she couldn't go home, her husband was jealous.

Seeing that the woman was not to be persuaded, Meg went to her own house; she could at least fetch some towels so that the woman could get dry. Indoors, as she went to the airing cupboard, she told her husband about the woman sitting on the wall in her soaking nightdress. But when she went back outside with the towels, the woman was gone.

'We knew her,' chorused several people in the group.

Jasper nodded significantly. There had indeed been a murder in the close. A while before Meg and her husband had moved there, a woman had gone missing. Her body had been found in the river a couple of days later by police divers. The following year, her husband was convicted of strangling her and dumping her body in the river.

A year or so after I heard the story from Jasper, the subject of Greenland Mills came up in conversation with a colleague in

Bath. I mentioned the ghost story. My colleague nodded; his neighbours had known the couple concerned. 'They were swopping,' he said. 'But it got out of control.'

7

THE CHOKING HAND

This second story from Bradford-on-Avon was told directly to Jasper by a member of the family concerned. This time, we were in the Shambles, a cobbled passageway in the centre of the town which had been the market in medieval times, standing in front of a narrow half-timbered building that had become a café.

In the first few years of this century, a young family moved from a big city to Bradford-on- Avon. The following summer, keen to show off the pretty country town they'd made their home, the couple invited their relatives to visit. And so it was that a large family group were having tea in one of the quaintest buildings in the town, and one of them took a photo to reserve the memory of the happy occasion.

Suddenly, the three year old started choking. Assuming a bit of dry biscuit had got stuck in her throat, her parents gave her a thump on the back. And then another one. But nothing came out, and now the child was visibly choking.

One parent put their fingers in the child's throat to loosen the obstruction but found nothing. Then they turned her upside down. Still nothing. The little girl was blue in the face and struggling for breath. One of the party happened to be a paramedic and performed the Heimlich manoeuvre, encircling the child and thumping her back. But nothing came out of her mouth and still she choked.

Meanwhile, someone had called an ambulance. In those days, there was a hospital on the road to Bath at the top of the town and the ambulance came quickly. The little girl was carried to the end of pedestrian passageway to be put into it. And then, as often happens once you've called the emergency services, she suddenly took a breath and was fine.

Some time afterwards, the person who'd taken the picture of the group taking tea had the photo developed. (In those days, you did that.) On the image, over the little girl's throat, was a white streak. Something dangled beneath it: Jasper had seen the photo blown up, and it resembled nothing so much as a dangling sleeve.

He paused. According to historical records, one Thomas Mayhew had been incarcerated for child murder in the building next to the cafe, the former town prison. Mayhew was a known dandy and liked to wear ornate white shirts with long dangling sleeves. Before he was hung in 1706, he sent for his best shirt from his hometown of Frome.

On a previous ghost walk, Jasper went on, someone smoking outside a nearby building had overheard the story and come over. She used to work in the bakery, said the local woman, and had seen something like a sleeve coming out of the wall. It was widely agreed among the bakery staff that the building was haunted and only the owner was willing to stay there alone after dark.

8

PISTOLS AT DAWN

It was Halloween in Bath, and a particularly pretty night. A bright three-quarter moon hung high in a clear sky, illuminating the outlines of the Georgian buildings as I joined a group outside the Theatre Royal for a ghost walk.

We were a small group: a family of five, a couple, and me. 'I'm brave,' confided the nine-year-old to the guide. Our guide certainly looked the part, a middle-aged man wearing a long black cape and top hat. We set off, pausing in front of various buildings to hear of a woman gliding through walls here, the sound of invisible children there. The guide maintained a good balance between scariness and reassurance and I was enjoying myself. It was pleasant, walking around on this mild evening, getting a different perspective on a city better known for its golden stone and tourists.

At the steps leading up to Victoria Park, the guide stopped again. Two men were often seen in this area, he said, who didn't fit into the life of the contemporary city. One was a flamboyant character dressed in the garb of the eighteenth century: a gold-embroidered jacket, knickerbocker trousers, stockings and buckled shoes. On his head sat a powered wig.

The other man's smart black suit was more modern but there was something about its cut and fabric that suggested a previous a era, perhaps the 1930s. According to those who had seen him, this second man, who was in his sixties, 'liked to be seen' and was given to appearing and disappearing in front of people's eyes. On one previous tour, he had been seen by nearly every member of the group.

'I'm forty per cent sure I've seen him myself,' the guide told us. His tone had departed from that of the professional tour guide and expressed genuine curiosity. 'He's walked past me. He looked exactly like the description I've heard and his suit didn't look contemporary.' He paused. 'On the other hand, he could just be an ordinary person, wearing different clothes. I still haven't decided.'

We climbed the steps and turned into the park. After following the path a little way, the group came to a stop in a dip in the lawn. Here, the guide told us, a man was often seen at arriving at first light. But he had never been seen walking away. A couple of centuries ago, the dell had served as a duelling ground and it was said that one morning, two duellers, their seconds and a doctor had gathered there. Of the five, only four survived. The doctor had taken the fatally wounded man into the shelter of a nearby holly tree for emergency treatment, but his efforts had been in vain. Visiting psychics said that the place was a 'psychic pool' that held the energy of violence and untimely death; some claimed to have seen streaks and balls of light.

Soon after the guide started speaking, I had moved out of the dip and back onto the higher ground of the path. My stomach was knotting and I had strong urge to cry. As people asked questions, controlling the nausea and the feeling in my throat was became increasingly difficult. I just wanted to leave.

The guide pointed to the holly tree, inviting members of the group to enter the leafy dome. 'Some people say it's warm in there; some say they get a strong negative feeling, some a positive one from touching the trunk,' he said, adding: 'I haven't been in there for a long time.'

I looked at the tree. Through a gap in its dense roundness I could see a space that resembled a small room. But there was no way I was going in, given how I was feeling. One of the group ducked under its canopy but came straight out again. Finally we were moving off, heading out of the park. It took a few minutes for the feeling of nausea to go.

The next morning, I was teaching not far from the park. The sun was out and my mood buoyant so at lunchtime I returned to the dell, curious to see how it felt in the practical light of day. Perhaps the uncomfortable feelings of the night before were down to the darkness and misty chill that had lain over the park. This time, I walked into the dell without difficulty; there was no feeling of repulsion and my head felt clear. Then I went and stood on the spot that I hadn't been able remain on the night before. And felt. There it was, that same clenching, churning in my stomach. It was as if my gut sensed something that my head didn't. The feeling spread upwards to my throat. Now I had a strong compulsion to gulp.

Enough. I returned to the sunlit path and walked quickly back to my place of work.

PART IV: QUANTUM TIMES

Our everyday experience suggests that time is linear and that generations live successively in places. But what if, as quantum physics has it, time was better understood in terms of layers or parallels? And what if experience depends, at least in part, on the state of our consciousness? This group of stories speaks to the intimate relationship between past and present.

9
ALICE IN SPIRITLAND

There's nothing as clichéd as a haunted house, depicted in novels and movies by ghosts holding severed heads and clanking chains. But what's it really like to live in a house inhabited by spirits? My friend Alice knows.

From the moment Alice set foot in the house, she felt an instant connection. The stone built cottage had barely been touched since the 1970s when it had been bought by its previous owner, a single woman without much money. There was no heating except storage heaters, and its ill-fitting windows were falling out of their frames.

The flowery wallpaper in the living room was almost the same as what Alice had grown up with in, while the main bedroom was a parody of seventies extravaganza. Flowers of the deepest pink cavorted up and down the walls, the woodwork was pink, and so was the carpet. Alice stood on the spot and laughed her head off. In the second bedroom, her hand went up to the polystyrene tiles on the ceiling. She wanted to pull them off, to start the work of bringing the house out of its time warp and into the present.

The estate agent was astonished when she came downstairs and put in an offer straightaway. 'Good lord!' he expostulated.

Alice could afford to buy the house and get it to twenty-first century standards, just, by doing the less skilled work herself. It had been built in the 1800s if not earlier and had originally been two tiny cottages, each with a fireplace for warmth and cooking and an upstairs room in which to sleep. One section had been extended in the 1960s and there was a big garden in which the original owners must have grown food. The bundle of old title deeds sent by the solicitor showed that the property had changed hands many times in the early twentieth century and that a rector from a nearby town had bought the cottage in 1952 for £450, selling it for only fifty pounds eleven years later.

Back in the twenty-first century, the renovation went swimmingly. The local tradesmen Alice hired turned out to be skilled and conscientious, full of suggestions and solutions for the various challenges presented by the hotchpotch cottage. Within a few months, the house had been gutted and rewired, fitted with central heating and a new kitchen. All the windows had been replaced and a new one added to bring more light to a dark room. Alice began the task of decorating and adding furnishings to make the place comfortable.

All the while, she had a strong sense of inheritance. The paint on the garden shed took her back to her very early childhood, as did the plants in the garden. According to neighbours, the previous owner was an independent woman with lots of interests who had remained active until she died at home in her nineties. She was described variously as 'indomitable', 'robust' and 'like a nana'. She had a running feud with one neighbour and used to tell off another for bicycling too fast past the cottage.

Alice had planned to make the main bedroom her own. But in the event, she found she could not sleep there. It was as if a kind of forcefield was in operation that repelled her as soon as she opened the door. So she used it as a store room and, when she went in to leave or fetch something, she made it quick. She often found herself singing as she did so, as the sound seemed to displace the energy and provide her with a protective bubble. She told a a visiting friend about the problem. 'Power!' said the friend when she opened the door to that room.

So Alice slept in the second bedroom. But even there, she sometimes had a sense of being watched at night and woke with the feeling that someone was standing at the end of the room. At others, exhausted after the day's physical work, she would fall asleep on the sofa before bedtime, to be suddenly awoken by the sound of ringing or of three knocks. Both came from the main bedroom.

Perhaps surprisingly, Alice wasn't particularly alarmed by these experiences. She had been sensitive to atmosphere all her life and was accustomed to places having very different feelings. From there, it was a short step to accept that the people and events of the past left residues, imprints that made up the character of the place and did no harm. It made sense that the previous owner might still be around and, given the age of the house, some of its previous occupants too. The building had been unoccupied for a while: from the outset Alice had a sense of spirits scattering in the way that spiders and other insects do when disturbed by a human. At first they might resent her presence but in time, things would settle down.

So she tolerated the spirits of the cottage. Fair enough. They could co-exist.

But one morning as she sat up in bed, something hissed in her face. She felt its breath on her skin. This palpable sign of hostility crossed a red line: action was required. Alice rang a man in a nearby town who advertised house clearings. Would he come over and do a clearance? The man talked to her kindly for some time. 'I don't get the feeling,' he said in his crystal-cut Queen's English,''that this is serious. I think you can clear the house yourself, but you need to be firmer.' He advised her on how to do a full clearance ritual, going into every corner of every room, declaring: 'This is my space. Go to the light!'

Alice did as he said and the activity of the house diminished. The forcefield in the pink bedroom, now re-plastered and painted white, had gone: it was now a pleasant, neutral space, full of light. Alice congratulated herself that she had prevailed and, a year after buying the house, finally moved into the main bedroom.

But once darkness fell, the sense of vigilance remained. Alice rarely slept well in the house and often woke to a feeling of relief that the night was over. She didn't usually suffer from nightmares, but one night she dreamt that something was on her throat. A picture appeared in her dreaming mind of a desiccated black rat; the rat had become part of her throat and needed to be scrapped out. On another occasion, she felt the body of a man lie down on the bed beside her. He was in a deep sleep and Alice tried, in her own sleep, to tell him to wake up. But he wouldn't and, in desperation, still asleep herself, she shouted 'WAKE UP!' and the man immediately disappeared.

A few moments later, there was a crash in the room and Alice woke up for real. The mirror above the chest of drawers had fallen off the wall, taking a few things with it.

Nothing was broken. But Alice recalled the dream she'd been having before the nightmare had begun. She was telling a figure on the other side of the bed that she'd swopped the mirror and the picture around, and that was why he couldn't see himself.

'Ghost busting takes time,' advised a psychic friend. 'You have to keep at it.' Another intuitive friend who stayed in the house while Alice was away reported having seen a figure by the window of the main bedroom. She also sensed a feeling of poverty and struggle in the house and surrounding land. 'Just think what people round here in the past had to do to get through their lives here,' she said.

In time, Alice moved out of the house for personal, non-supernatural reasons and the difficult nights stopped.

10

HISTORICAL SLIPS

This is not so much a story as a 'little seeing', one of the supernatural experiences that are quite commonly reported and neither taken particularly seriously nor roundly dismissed by the world at large. This one testifies to the power of the in-between states of consciousness that facilitate them, the hypnogogic and hynopompic states that mark the threshold between sleep and wakefulness. A soft sideways gaze, according to seekers of such experiences, is important: stare straight at a spirt and it will likely disappear!

My godmother had recently moved to Dorset and was doing the rounds to get to know people, attending local events in the surrounding villages. One day she went to a talk in the Old Chapel in East Stour, a chunk of a brick building that had been built as a place of nonconformist worship in the nineteenth century.

The old meeting house still had its pews and the light that filtered through the narrow perpendicular windows was dim. The talk was dull and, despite the hardness of the seating, my godmother dozed off. When she opened her eyes, the first thing she saw was a little old lady in a bonnet and a long brown dress. The lady was sitting in a pew just in front to the right of her, and was leaning forward in an attitude of devotion.

'Ah, yes,' was my godmother's immediate thought. She intuitively understood that the old lady wasn't a member of the audience and belonged to the past. Despite never having had any experience of the supernatural, in her sleepy, relaxed state she felt no surprise.

And then suddenly the old lady wasn't there.

Years later, my godmother and I drove past the chapel. Like many former schools and churches in the English countryside, it had by that time been converted in a family home. 'I wonder if they've seen the Victorian lady?' said my godmother.

∼

Some friends of my godmother's reacted with a similar lack of surprise when they encountered a figure from the past.

The couple, who were in their thirties and described by my godmother as 'not fanciful', were walking near the estate of Kingston Lacy. They were enjoying the Dorset landscape with its open fields and vast skies and, as they continued down past the country house and over the down lands, they passed another man on the path. They both accepted him as just another person you see when out for a walk.

But the next moment the realisation sunk in: the man they had just passed was a Roman soldier.

Now they were surprised, and turned around to take a better look. But the man was gone.

The couple had been walking near the Roman settlement of Vindocladia which had been established around 44 BC as the Romans advanced through southern Britain. The remains of that time include the Shapwick Roman Fort and evidence of what may have been a Roman amphitheatre.

11

OLD WOMAN KNITTING

It was almost Halloween and fifteen friends and neighbours were standing around the fire pit at the bottom of my garden. The night sky was big and dark, we'd had sausages and cake, and now it was time for the telling of tales. Looking round the circle, I asked whether anyone knew any ghost stories.

'I've got a ghost story,' said Sophie immediately.

Sophie, a lively young woman who hailed from Wales, lived a few doors down. The gathered circle pricked up its ears and, with smiling confidence, Sophie began her story.

As a little girl of around five, she would often go and visit her grandfather. He lived on a council estate in south Wales in a terraced house with a big back garden. She had a twin sister but, for reasons she didn't make clear, was often played alone in the garden. And it was there, looking back towards the house, that she had a clear view of the living room window and that of the room next to it.

As she went about her play, Sophie often saw an old woman in the window of this second room. The woman was sitting in one of those big bamboo chairs with a rounded back and was covered in blankets. And she was always knitting: knitting, knitting, knitting. Sophie would wave to her and the old woman would wave back with the exaggerated enthusiasm older people often put on for small children.

Time went by, and Sophie continued to see the woman knitting in the window when she played in her grandfather's garden. One day, when her childlike acceptance had given way to the curiosity of an older child, she mentioned her to her grandfather. Who was she? She never saw her anywhere else except in the window. Her grandfather started at the question. There was no old woman there, he replied.

But his granddaughter insisted that there was, and gave a detailed description of the woman she had seen so many times.

At this, her grandfather's face broke into a smile. 'That's your great-grandmother,' he said. 'She died a few months before you and your sister were born. She knew you were coming, and was knitting clothes for you.'

When she shared her experiences with her twin, Sophie learnt that her sister had also seen the old woman knitting.

❧ 12 ❧

AFTER-DEATH APPEARANCES

I've often found that when I ask someone if they've ever seen a ghost, the immediate response is 'no'. Sometimes this is followed by a pause or a few moments in which the conversation proceeds in a different direction and then suddenly the person remembers an encounter with the supernatural. I put this temporary amnesia partly down to our materialist culture and partly down to clichéd perceptions of what constitutes a ghost.

Mary is an extreme example of this phenomenon. She remained convinced she'd never seen a ghost for years, despite having seen several dead people she knew. And one day she finally realised: that's exactly what ghosts are!

It was a bright sunny morning and Mary was taking advantage of a practical mood to give the house a good clean. She opened the door to shake out the duster. There on the path was Betty, standing in front of the house next door as if about to knock. 'Oh hello,' said Mary. She said it in her head because she knew Betty had recently died. The news had not come as a surprise: the sixty-something woman had been suffering from cancer for some time, and the steady deterioration of her health had been obvious to everyone in the local community. Seeing Betty standing there, albeit looking somewhat see-through, was a reminder that today was the day of her funeral, which Mary had decided not to attend.

'Go well, Betty,' said Mary out loud and closed the door. Then she went to check the time. It was exactly midday, the time the funeral was due to start in the church down the road. That explained it. Mary got back to her cleaning and thought no more of the incident.

For Mary, this was an 'ordinary seeing', part of the texture of reality of the time and place in which she was living. She was accustomed to the sights and sounds of the spirit world, so it was hardly surprising that someone who had lived nearby should re-materialise soon after their death. But seeing the departed in physical form was a fairly new experience for her. They were exactly as they had been when alive, except for the fact they were semi-translucent, as if projected onto a screen. The visiting dead were neither 'out there' in the normal sense, nor in the private world of her imagination: the 'seeing' took place somewhere in-between.

The first time she'd seen a dead person was more as you would expect, an experience intertwined with feelings of sadness and significance. She was visiting a friend who had suffered a tragedy: the suicide of her partner and father of her young child. Mary was accompanying her friend, the couple's small child and the dead man's uncle as they made a little pilgrimage to the place of death. The young man had hung himself amid the trees in a local beauty spot near a lake.

The little group wound its way through the woods: a large man, a little boy and the two women, one bearing a big bunch of red roses. Their mood was calm and matter-of-fact as they negotiated the narrow path, pointing out dips and trips to each other. 'Here we are,' said the widow after ten minutes, and the group came to a halt. Beside the path was a good-sized tree – was it an oak? with a nice big trunk and some thick branches that spread out over the path. Mary stood staring ahead as her friend gave a few details of the death. Yes, it was one of his favourite places. Yes, his body had been found by walkers. No, not very nice for them.

But it was hard to concentrate on what her friend was saying because Mary was watching the fifth figure in front of her. Soon after the group had come to a standstill, a form had slipped out of the tree, as if detaching itself from the trunk. Mary recognised him at once: his long brown hair was tied back in the way she remembered from her few meetings with him and he was wearing a cosy blue hoodie and jeans. He seemed very much at ease, and his face wore a gentle smile as he circled the space beneath the tree. He was clearly pleased to have visitors and was welcoming them as best he could.

Then somehow there were just four people again and none of them had much to say. Mary's friend placed the roses in a hole in the tree that was just at the right height, and they made their way back along the path, their thoughts turning to what they would cook for the evening meal.

Mary said nothing to her friend about what she had seen. She figured that even if her experience was taken seriously, it would not be helpful: wouldn't you be jealous if someone else saw your dead beloved?

The next time she saw a dead person, Mary knew beyond any doubt that her experience would be completely dismissed by the person she was with.

She had gone with a friend to visit a new grave. In it lay the body of a mutual friend, a man who had died of cancer in middle age. Neither Mary nor her friend had been able to attend the funeral, although they had badly wanted to, and the trip to the graveside was intended as their own private rite of grief. Mary's friend – let's call her Ella – was particularly upset. Initially, Mary had been surprised when Ella begged to be taken to the grave as soon as possible. Officially, she was the strictest of atheists, someone who believed that science and physical evidence contained all the truth worth knowing; she had little time for the spiritual. But realising that Ella had a deeper need for the rituals of mourning than she would admit, Mary put aside a weekend to drive them both to the church.

Their dead friend – let's call him Peter – was buried in a coastal village he'd been fond of, although he'd never lived there. The day of the expedition was a Sunday in winter and, as a storm was brewing, the two women hoped to complete their journey before the weather broke. After a windy drive across country, the pair found the church without difficulty. But there were several graves too new to be marked in the churchyard and they had to ask the churchwarden to show them which one it was.

Peter had been popular: shells pressed into the sides of the sandy mound spoke of other recent visitors. The two friends crouched by the grave. Ella seemed very sad, and Mary wanted to comfort her with her sense that Peter wasn't really under the earth in the way she believed. But she had known her companion a long time and knew better than to say such a thing.

The pair decided to go to the beach, which was just a short walk down a slipway outside the churchyard. The promised storm was brewing and everything – sky, sea and sand – was grey-brown. They walked slowly to the sand's end where the little bay was bounded by some low cliffs. Ella picked up some shells as the tide swirled around the muddy rock pools and stood staring silently at the horizon.

After lingering a while longer, the women turned back with thoughts of lunch at the village pub. A good few yards separated them as they wound their way along the sand and Mary suddenly became conscious that Peter was there in the space, walking between them. She could see his translucent body but not discern the expression on his face. Yet his presence emanated a calm delight and the sense of him meandering along the beach with them was so strong that Mary would not have stepped into the space for fear of bumping into him.

As the three arrived at the foot of the slipway, Mary felt Peter stop. He was staying on the beach. Instinctively, as she and Ella walked up the slope, she turned and gave him a discreet wave. At Ella's request, they returned to the grave where she pressed the shells she'd collected into the sand and whispered something to the head end of the mound. Mary felt an internal jolt of surprise: didn't Ella know that Peter was not there but living happily on the beach?

In the pub, Sunday lunch was in full swing. Families and couples filled the wooden tables, talking and eating with gusto. After the long drive and emotional morning, the two women were hungry and pleased when generous platefuls of food were placed in front of them.

Mary was tucking into her roast beef and Yorkshire pudding when she felt a kind of bump across the table. Peter had just sat down in the seat diagonally opposite, although this time she couldn't see him at all. 'Oh, are you here too?' She asked him mentally.

'Of course I'm having lunch with you,' came the reply. Then the din of the pub rose and Mary was drawn back into the business of eating and the people around her. The drive home was uneventful and the women got home before the storm broke.

PART V: AND FINALLY …

13

THE GHOST'S TAIL

If dead people can pop back to visit the earthly realm, can animals?

A cousin of mine was having coffee with someone she didn't know very well. As she sat in the kitchen while her hostess prepared their drinks, a small black cat walked across the room and disappeared as though through a cat-flap. The cat was distinctive-looking, with one white foot and a tail that went straight up with a kink at the end. It wore a red collar.

Surprised, she described the cat to her hostess. 'That's Binkie!' cried the other woman in delight. Her beloved cat had died some eight years previously. Going to the other side of the kitchen, she pulled back a curtain to reveal Binkie's old cat-flap.

Then she went and found out a photo to show my cousin. And sure enough, there was a black cat in a red collar with one white foot and a tail with a kink at the end.

ABOUT THE AUTHOR

Dr Alex Klaushofer is an author and journalist who has written extensively on social and affairs and politics in Britain and Middle East. Her work has appeared in publications such as *The Guardian* and *The Daily Telegraph*, along with contributions to BBC radio.

Her books combine reportage, travel writing and one or two other genres. *Paradise Divided* tells the human stories of modern-day Lebanon and explores the mix of social, religious and political forces that make up this complex country.

The Secret Life of God is a kind of spiritual investigation into twenty-first century Britain which chronicles how, in an ostensibly secular age, people are finding new ways of believing and belonging.

She writes essays about the changing times on Substack at Ways of Seeing: www.alexklaushofer.substack.com. Her website can be found at: www.alexklaushofer.com.

www.ingramcontent.com/pod-product-compliance
Lightning Source LLC
Chambersburg PA
CBHW070441010526
44118CB00014B/2135